Zero Degrees

poems by

Helen Marie Casey

Finishing Line Press
Georgetown, Kentucky

Zero Degrees

Copyright © 2018 by Helen Marie Casey
ISBN 978-1-63534-435-6 First Edition
All rights reserved under International and Pan-American Copyright Conventions. No part of this book may be reproduced in any manner whatsoever without written permission from the publisher, except in the case of brief quotations embodied in critical articles and reviews.

ACKNOWLEDGMENTS

These narrative poems would not exist were it not for the brave journalists around the world who report out to the rest of us the stories of atrocities perpetrated by one or more humans against others. I thank these brave witnesses who put their life on the line so that we may know what might otherwise forever remain hidden and unacknowledged.

To all those writers who have provided workshops which inspired me, including Carolyn Forche, David Mason, Timothy Liu, the late Carolyn Kizer, and the late Ruth Whitman, my deepest gratitude. I could never have entered the stream of Poetry of Witness without the many predecessors who have carved a path.

My most important and my first reader and critic remains my husband Dean. I thank him from the bottom of my heart as I do my large family and circle of friends for their curiosity about and support of what my writing life leads to. In particular, I thank the following writers who have provided counsel, critiques, encouragement, and substantive suggestions: Patti Marxsen, Anita Kurth, Moira Linehan Ounjian, the late Brian Doyle, Tom Daley, Barbara Helfgott Hyett, and my writing circle, the Monday Poets, Anita Ouellette, Joel Moskowitz, Lee Mendenhall, Linda Havel, Ellen Jane Powers, Dawn Randall, and Sherri Stepakoff, as well as those who have led the way, Ruth Harriet Jacobs, Rhea Sossen, Isabel Ferguson, and Emma Zevik.

Publisher: Leah Maines
Editor: Christen Kincaid
Cover Art: Tacha Vosburgh, Tachavosburgh@msn.com
Author Photo: Art Illman, www.artillman.com
Cover Design: Elizabeth Maines McCleavy

Printed in the USA on acid-free paper.
Order online: www.finishinglinepress.com
          also available on amazon.com

                    Author inquiries and mail orders:
                          Finishing Line Press
                            P. O. Box 1626
                        Georgetown, Kentucky 40324
                               U. S. A.

Table of Contents

Zero Degrees 1

Our Girls 2

About the Murdered Boy 3

It Begins with Ink 4

Soliloquy on Zareena's Ghost 5

The Writing Lesson 6

Rukshana 7

An Etymological Riff 8

Farkhunda 9

For Kayla 10

Man in a Cage 11

Palmyra's Antiquities 12

Bataclan Theater 13

15th of April 2013 14

Killing Saba 16

Expectant 17

Felled 18

There were Nineteen of Them 19

A Pakistani Girl's Story 20

The Murdered Women 22

Always for my best friend, Dean

Zero Degrees

Color of pearl, afternoon's snow, sky, and horizon overlap,
sift into mounds and heaps, delicate contours, frozen pools
like mirrors, but more treacherous. Nights, wind heaves
against the crested snow. Elsewhere, across the waters,
in Denmark, France, Nigeria, Libya, bullets and knives
search out targets, terror everywhere. Hate masked.

Winter and summer and again winter and summer, without end,
as if all the burning, shooting, maiming, and threatening can never
be enough. Extermination is missionary, is the purpose of war, precisely
down to zero, not even one left to keen or pray or return fire.

Evil metastasizes, one military cell not content until it spreads.
Knives. Machetes. Kalishnikovs. Explosives. Infernos. Hooded,
the mind-riddled march, darkness wherever they stomp.
Their boots fill with the blood of those they extinguish. Sky
withdraws. Even the landscape shudders. It wants to turn away.

Zero degrees where I live. At my window, I stand searching.
An eight-point buck, one doe, and then another, partly concealed
among the trees. The snow a kind of shelter. I think they are not afraid.
Nothing they know tells them to flee into another land.
Nothing tells them the truth about fire power.
Nothing tells them there is no way to prepare.

Our Girls
Nigeria: April 14, 2014

My girl is not afraid. She is seldom mute or glum.
No one drags her from school. No guns in her face.
She can laugh and play and sing and walk alone,
wear short skirts, her toes naked in sandals, scarlet polish
on her nails. She does not cover her dark, dark hair, loose
at her neck. This innocent child is licking frosting
from her fine, long fingers, her tongue happy.
She is deciding which book to read, which song to sing,
which assignment to complete. She does not conceive
of any other life, does not believe in unrelieved malice.

I am listening, listening to the loud refrain:
Bring back our girls. More than 200 of them
stolen, covered up now in burqas. Terrified.
Mute. Their eyes alone can speak for them.
The girls are lonely for everyone except their captors.
They are lonely for mother and father. They are missing
sister, brother, home, embers where they cook manioc,
yam, plantain, chicken; they are missing the well, place
of gathering, where they cup water. They lament sky
above Chibok which, perhaps, they may never see again.
They are lonely for no one but those they love. And books.

About the Murdered Boy

I grew to look forward to it, the rain hitting the porch
like hail, the presence of something not myself
doing what it was given to do. I could go a long time
thinking the earth at peace with itself.
Then comes thunder. One boy stabs another.
I'd prefer to say the earth groans. It doesn't.
Winter earth grows a hard shell.
No sound penetrates.

It Begins with Ink
Paris, January 2015

Carnage coming. Cold and rainy.
A threatening day.
Pens and pencils in place,
team of compatriots reviewing
designs. They have been attacked
before. And lived. Taken by surprise
this time. Two gunmen, Kalishnikovs ready,
enter, address the victims by name,
begin to shoot. *I would rather die standing
than live on my knees.* And then they fall,
journalists, cartoonists, editors, police officer,
papers, blood, the floor afloat. Outside,
Everything all right, Boss, and then, defensive,
hands raised, police officer down. Shot
in the head. Next day, another officer killed.
Point blank. Search continues. Darkness falls
on the forest. Helicopters. Armor. Dogs.
Weapons. Vincennes, near Charles DeGaulle,
print shop taken by two killers, Saïd and Chérif.
Words under attack. Images critical.
Elsewhere, hostages in jeopardy. Courage.
Some fall, protecting others. In the *Hyper Cacher,*
bullets, explosions, fear on the shelves
and in the aisles. Customers become stories.
One man hides others, then goes for help.
Four die. At length, the terrorists, including Khibali,
shot dead. Who is there that mourns such men,
mad dogs among us? *Je suis Charlie,
je suis Ahmed,* the people shout.
They embrace policemen. Pencils rise.
Pens are clenched in fists and then they, too,
rise. Children march. Parents march
and sing. Soon, books and placards rise.
Millions of books grow feet and hands.
They sing at the top of their lungs.
They sing the *Marseillaise* and pump their fists.

Soliloquy on Zareena's Ghost

When the soldiers executed her for her crime, it was
in a stadium so thousands could see exactly what there was
to see of Zareena, mother of seven. One might imagine
he had it coming, her husband, or why would she
have killed him, knowing she could not run? Did he
beat her one time too many, was that it?

After they took her down from the back of the pickup truck,
they walked her away from the women who accompanied her.
She knelt in the open, surrounded by eyes, thousands of them.
Was there any doubt in her mind about what would happen
when the men with weapons moved too close to her?

She was as still and docile as she could be. They shot her
in the head. Right in the back of the head. She fell
the way the executed do, her burqa absolutely still.
Afterward, the Taliban who lifted her body from the ground
drove her away. It was said the husband's family had already
forgiven her and she should not have been killed. What
about her children, what do they say of this shooting?
Must they, too, be still as night?

The keep of my mind grows still and I hear Zareena
calling her sisters to her, one brave woman, invisible,
filming it all. Now why would she dare such a thing?
If there is a record of an event, does it prove
the event happened just exactly as it did?

Yet, there is no image of the tears that drenched them,
the women who had already begun to mourn.

The Writing Lesson
       October 1, 2015   Roseburg, Oregon

A morning like any other morning
except it wasn't like any other
logging roads waiting
English teacher waiting
students in place
killer coming in the door
what is going to happen waits
Grandma, he killed my teacher
I saw it
he killed nine before
he killed himself, perhaps thinking
of his mother who used to
shoot with him.

Heroes among the dead
and injured, fear and lack
of comprehension
murder and mayhem always
incomprehensible,
Oregon lumber loaded on rigs
bass running , spirits of the Umpqua
and Calapuya silently watching, perhaps
today's lesson meant to be introductory
paragraphs and sequences:
beginning, middle, end, all of it
with a sense of inevitability.

Rukhshana
Kabul, October 2015

When it is over, who will remember Rukhshana,
young and beautiful, a girl who could read?
Was it reading that undid her, taught her to dream,
to think she could control her own life, make decisions?
Nineteen years old when she was stoned to death,
the pit freshly dug and deep, her head visible, eyes terrified,
a target for men who hated her defiance. What right
did she think she had to choose her own man?
She prayed aloud to Allah as the men lusted after what?
Her body? Her blood? Her death? Her annihilation?

The man they called her lover, Mohammad Gul, flogged,
one hundred lashes that, when it was over, did not want to heal,
the way memory does not want to let go of what it knows.
In Kabul, Rukhshana's mother rocks and cries,
She was part of my body. And now the mother has her daughter,
bloodied and dead, in her arms, women wailing, afraid.
What is there to say when killers do not pay, mothers mourn,
fathers curse, and nothing changes? Allah is nowhere near.
Perhaps he wants nothing more to do with Kabul.
Perhaps he was not listening as Rukhshana begged,
or he was, and looked away.

An Etymological Riff on Two Brothers Who Planted Bombs
Boston Marathon   April 15, 2013

Turmoil sounds like but is not turf or soil or smurf or oil.
Tears oil our cheeks, roil our soul, tear our turf.
Ur-sacrifice: child on the pyre, unsaved.
Toil and moil: the drudgery of everyday labor,
not intended as bombs in our rubbish cans,
not as limbs sundered on a marathon route.
Molestation or misery: Ainsworth on *moil,*
spelled also *m-o-y-l-e.* And in 1659, Hammond:
Their life for that space was hard travail or moyle.
Mrs. Browning, wife of Robert, in 1856, of those
dead of plague: *The moil of death upon them.*
She could not have anticipated 2013, two hundred sixty
directly injured, three dead, one more murdered in Cambridge,
the moil of death upon them. Transitive verb, *to moil:*
to root up; to burrow in like a pig, badger, etc. To burrow
like a bomber, backpack in place of shovels. Or tunnels.
Tur: A greyish-brown wild goat, native to southeastern Russia,
sounds like but is not *turd,* a word no longer in polite use, meaning
excrement, ordure, applied to a person as a term of contempt.

Farkhunda
Murdered in Kabul, March 2015

Who can believe it possible about sane men,
the woman only 27 years old, that they should lie,
stomp the woman to death, throw her body off a roof,
run over her with a car, set her broken body ablaze?

Who can believe it possible, in Kabul, women bear
the weight of the coffin, carry it through the streets,
not one man allowed to touch what remains of her?

Who can believe it possible Farkhunda does not die,
her spirit insistent, coming to inhabit these women
dressed entirely in black, venomous, black widows
who will, it is said, on occasion eat the male after mating.

For Kayla
>*Captured by ISIS in 2013. Killed 2015.*

What can one say to the dead whose suffering
grew larger every day, new pain rising on top of old?
What can the dead hear that matters to them?
Before they die, do they despair of final justice?
Do they come to think living with pain and fear
is forever, fear undiminished? Do the women
who are raped, whose parts are brutally opened
and penetrated, over and over and over again, dream
of revenge? Do they fantasize their retribution, how
they would castrate these men, blades red-hot,
sharper than any earthly weapon, how they would
watch them bleed and scream for mercy, slice and dice
the testes, then the erect penis in their hands, in the end,
feed the bloody eviscerated parts to each cadaverous man?
Do the women watch for one flicker of comprehension
among these men? Or do they not believe regret possible
in soldiers like these, more brute than human?
Perhaps they do not believe a soul inhabits the bodies
of such men. Perhaps they tell themselves there is no other
explanation for the cruelty, save that they were
devils incarnate, but how can that be?

Man in a Cage
    Islamic State Executes Jordanian Pilot

It would not, could not end well. Captors hungry for vengeance,
their jaws set, eyes bouncing in and out of focus, pilot young, bruised,
their doomed prey. This is sport, their captive less than dirt except
for what they will do to him. He can no longer fight back.
No more plane. No more bombs. Not one dagger in his hands.
Sands of the desert begin to stir. An updraft. Gaze of the sun steady.
If the band of soldiers hesitates, they, too—all of them—will be caged,
or so they may believe.

Masked except their eyes, the soldiers grow skittish before
they light the fuse, flames running toward him, their victim
alone in the slatted cage, human animal, screaming, nowhere to run,
no shield from the flames that will consume him until
he is reduced, cinders where once there was a man,
pawn in their contest. And then a bulldozer to annihilate
all trace of this particular enemy.
                                            What will his dear mother
and father never say of this blazing day, words inadequate,
heart of their Qur'an defiled, the prophet mocked?
And the wife, the young wife, hair veiled, tears
tracking her face, images she sees corrosive,
what can she hope? Time, unheeding.
Face of stone.

Palmyra's Antiquities

Old, revered, he was like an antiquity himself. Little
wonder they did what they did to Khalid al-Asaad.
They tried hard to destroy him, thinking the loss
of his grizzled head would teach him a thing or two.
They hung his body, bloody, headless, by his wrists,
above his severed head, his glasses intact. He had
refused to hide himself, refused to leave Palmyra,
refused to tell what they wanted to know:
Where are they, the hidden treasures?
He took his secrets with him, blood splattering
the trail. Perhaps it is he who will prevail.

Militants think a ruin they detonate cannot be re-born.
They are convinced public execution works
to make cowards of us all. Don't they know anything
about the staying power of the executed, how a story
finds its path and circulates the way feet never can?
We know Khalid al-Assad's name. The man who
killed him, do we care to know his name?

Bataclan Theater
      Paris: November 2015

They shot us like birds
until they, too, became prey
we were nothing to them
but targets
nothing resembling hate
in them, nor remorse,
not one soul among them
their minds empty
as feed bags
infected with vermin
bullets the only language
they they they they
until they destructed
blood-filled oblivion
dark, silent, lonely,
with no acclaim
none forever and ever.

15th of April 2013

Two dead, then three.
Twenty-three injured, then two hundred sixty.
Organized chaos, nurses report.
Then triage in medical tents.

Fairmont Copley locked down.
Fear of more bombs.
Witnesses can't explain exactly what happened.
After the second explosion, tears and fear.

Leads racked and stacked.
1-800-callFBI.
Black hat and white hat, bills backward. Fuzzy images.
Backpacks. Clear images.
Narrow casting nets terrorists.

Suspects foreign-born. In USA since 2000.
SUV carjacked. MIT officer killed. MBTA officer shot.
BU and BC closed.
Babson, MIT, Harvard closed.
Boston taxi service suspended.

"Don't answer the door."
SWAT and HAZMAT gear.
"All of Boston should now shelter in place."
Heightened security at Logan.
All public transportation halted.
Red Sox on hold.

UMass Dartmouth closed.
Lockdown in Boston, Watertown, Newton,
Brookline, Belmont, Waltham, Cambridge,
Allston/Brighton.

Shootout. Armored vehicles come and go.
Governor, Mayor, Police Chief lock down crime scene.
Controlled explosions in Cambridge.
Watertown. Night vision. ICE officers. Negotiators.

Blood everywhere.
Journalists. Digital cameras. Bullets flying.
Younger brother, 19 years old and 113 pounds,
drives over older brother to escape. Older brother dies.

Door-to-door searches.
Fruitless.

Younger killer detected in boat
dry-docked in backyard.
Apprehended.

All the victims random
and innocent
of everything but being there
Marathon Monday.

Killing Saba

After they shot her in the face
after they stuffed her in a bag
after they dropped her in a river,
night and the river dark as mud,
her father and uncle went home.
The men were proud, honor
restored, until the girl rose.
Undead. Scarred but not dead.
Bushes saved her, held her,
until she climbed back. Not
dead. Not silent. Pakistan awake.
Rules of honor unchanging.
She refuses forgiveness until
she can no longer resist. Freed,
her father boasts. He knows
he has done the right thing,
his family's honor essential,
her will, her decisions, her
right to choose, not. Not
in daylight, or moonlight,
not ever.

Expectant
    June 2016: Punjab Province

It is said the mother lured her daughter
who also was a mother, who already knew
another infant was coming, perhaps also a girl,
lured this mother-to-be into a snare—
this was in Butrawala village in Pakistan—
a snare from which she would not emerge,
no, she would never emerge and the blood
would keep flowing, pumping until deep red,
crusting, after her mother and brother slit
the throat of their own Muqadas Tofeeq,
twenty-two years old, whose once-beautiful
voice screamed until she choked and stopped,
no longer owning a voice or her body. She ceased
to be, this woman who married a man she chose,
a man with dark hair, a mustache, and courage.
He prays now, Mohammed Tofeeq, beside his wife's
grave, his daughter in his lap. She, too, this young
child, will learn to pray. She will visit again
and again the mound where her mother lies.
Perhaps she will want to burrow into it to hide
when she chooses her own man and marries him.

Felled

Horrific hurricane winds are on their way and I wonder, can they know, those skittery hummingbirds, insatiable as death, astride gangly asters?

Overhead, three hawks circle. Below them, one bold scarlet cardinal. Trees tremble as if they know. Abrupt shaking begins. Winds violent, as in violates what they will. I cancel my birthday.

Branches crack, hurl themselves. Sky, dullest gray, reaches toward charcoaled ebony. Rains do what rains do, pounding, pounding. White geraniums keel. Oaks, maples, and pines crash to earth, felled— like my friend Joan. Barely a sound as he choked the air away.

There Were Nineteen of Them
June 2016

One by one, until there were nineteen,
the Yezidi girls were shoved into cages,
like purloined bounty, waiting for exchange,
locked inside while hundreds gathered,
in Mosul, helpless to do anything but watch,
pickup trucks carrying iron cages of girls,
nineteen young girls. Head to toe, they wore
white—desert flowers with no oasis in sight—
implements for bonfires waiting to do the work
they must do, no resistance possible,
gasoline and matches suffocatingly ready
for flames devouring flesh and cloth, hair and veils,
stockings, gloves, shawls, shoes, undergarments,
smell of blacked, cooked flesh everywhere heavy.

When the immolation was complete, embers
remaining, nineteen consumed by flames,
hundreds who watched and could do nothing
to stop the deaths of nineteen girls, turned away
from the girls-turned-cinders, from the cries
they will never forget, from the soldiers who set
the fire, who perhaps shuddered like Ugolino before
he brought his face down, devouring his own sons.

Once there was a man, Muhammad Abdullah al-Jabouri.
He tried to help Yezidi girls escape. What happened
to him came swiftly. He knelt before them, crowds
silent, arms crossed. They watched the splatter,
praise of God hissing on the lips of the killers.

A Pakistani Girl's Story
April 2016

Before I was sentenced to die
in Abottabad, I went some years
to school. I could read
and write and came to know
my own mind.

I am Ambreen Riasat
sentenced to death
by the jirga, men
who decide about life
and death.

Kidnapped from my bed
by them, I was drugged
and dragged away.
I was strangled with ropes
then I was tied inside
the back seat of a van
where I was barely alive
when they set the fire
in the green hills
of Makol.

When my father found me
like a statue in the van
my fists clenched
cinders moved everywhere
on the metal seats.

Bangles lay where once
my arm had been
and in the wind
the question—
what had she
my mother
who never went
looking for me
said
or not said
when they asked
what I might have done.

The Murdered Women

They don't become angels, these murdered women, nor are they at peace.
I see all of them united, wherever they are, haunting the last place
they knew, fragments of his skin under their nails, eyes of the dead filled
with all the reasons these women do not wish to be angels, angels with no
bodies, who have never breathed, made love, worried about a lost child.
The murdered women I have known were, every one too young to die,
too much in love with life to lose it. In fact, they didn't lose their lives.
Their lives were stolen from them.
The murdered do not become angels whose whole existence has been
paradise, no dirty laundry, no cooking spice-filled meals, no mice in the
traps, no dog waiting to be rubbed, no rumpled bed, night,
its own pungent music, and dreams. The murdered are like the inflamed.
Their every thought is of return, sweet return, the memory of the final
moments engulfed not in forgiveness but in amber, a knowledge that can
never be erased.

Helen Marie Casey lives in Sudbury, Massachusetts, a small New England town settled in 1638. Her love of history led her to write a poetry chapbook, *Inconsiderate Madness*, about Quaker martyr Mary Dyer, hanged in 1660. The book won the Black River Chapbook Competition of Black Lawrence Press. Seven poems from the book were set to music and twice performed in Montana in 2007 as "A Flag for Others." Helen's poetry chapbook about the military figure Joan of Arc, *Fragrance upon His Lips*, had an early reading at Shakespeare & Company in Paris. Helen has also written a monograph, "Portland's Compromise: The Colored School 1867-1872," and a biography of a Sudbury painter, "My Dear Girl: The Art of Florence Hosmer." Her poetry and reviews have appeared in numerous journals and anthologies, including *Prairie Schooner, The Laurel Review, Paterson Literary Review, Comstock Review, Connecticut Review, Louisiana Literature, Calyx, The Worcester Review, The South Carolina Review*, and the anthology, *Lay Bare the Canvas: New England Poets on Art*. Helen won first prize in the 14th National Poet Hunt of the *MacGuffin* in 2010 and she won the Frank O'Hara Prize of the Worcester County Poetry Association in 2014. She was named a semifinalist for the 2015 Paumanok Poetry Award competition and she has been nominated for a Pushcart Prize. For many years her columns appeared in the *Metrowest Daily News* as well as in several regional publications. Her. B.A. in English and French is from the University of Portland and her M.A. in English from Portland State University. She also pursued doctoral work in Literary Studies at Washington State University.

www.ingramcontent.com/pod-product-compliance
Lightning Source LLC
LaVergne TN
LVHW040118080426
835507LV00041B/1724